SHERLOCK BONES LOOKS AT PHYSICAL SCIENCE

Magnets and Springs

Harriet McGregor

WINDMILL BOOKS
New York

Published in 2011 by Windmill Books, LLC
303 Park Avenue South, Suite #1280, New York, NY 10010-3657

First Edition

Senior Editor: Camilla Lloyd
Designer: Simon Borrough
Consultant: Jon Turney
Picture Researcher: Amy Sparks
Illustrator: Stefan Chabluk
Sherlock Bones Artwork: Richard Hook

Photographs:
Abbreviations: t-top, b-bottom, l-left, r-right, m-middle.
Cover: Dreamstime (Iofoto); **Insides: Folios** Dreamstime (Alst); **1** Getty (Diane
Collins and Jordan Hollender); **4** Photolibrary (Josh Westrich); **6** Dreamstime (Nrogel);
9 Science Photo Library (Andrew Lambert Photography); **12** Shutterstock (Andresr); **14**
Photolibrary (Ron Dahlquist); **15** Corbis (Martin Harvey); **16** Dreamstime (Holgs); **18**
Dreamstime (Alst); **19** Dreamstime (Sonyae); **20** Getty (Simon Watson); **21** Shutterstock
(Ilin Sergey); **22** Dreamstime (Alst); **23** (t) Dreamstime (Arthurdent), (b) Shutterstock
(Robert Pernell); **24** (l) Shutterstock (Sabri Deniz Kizil), (r) Shutterstock (Niderlander);
25 (t) Shutterstock (HomeStudio), (b) Corbis (Gideon Mendel); **26** Shutterstock
(Ahseng); **27** (l) Dreamstime (Eric1513), (inset) Dreamstime (Ctrphotos);
29 Shutterstock (Feng Yu).

Library of Congress Cataloging-in-Publication Data

McGregor, Harriet.
 Magnets and springs / by Harriet McGregor. — 1st ed.
    p. cm. — (Sherlock Bones looks at physical science)
 Includes index.
 ISBN 978-1-61533-213-7 (library binding)
 1. Magnets—Juvenile literature. 2. Magnetism—Juvenile literature. 3. Springs
(Mechanism)—Juvenile literature. I. Title.
 QC757.5.M38 2011
 538'.4—dc22
                          2010024565

Manufactured in China

For more great fiction and nonfiction, go to www.windmillbooks.com

CPSIA Compliance Information: Batch #WAW1102W: For Further Information contact Windmill Books, New York, New York on 1-866-478-0556.

Contents

Words that appear in **bold** can be found in the glossary on page 30.

The Science Detective, Sherlock Bones, will help you learn all about Magnets and Springs. The answers to Sherlock's questions can be found on page 31.

What Is Magnetism?

Magnetism is a type of **force**. A force is a push or a pull. We use pushes and pulls every day without even thinking about it. We push the covers off the bed in the morning, pull the bathroom door open, and pull the lid off of the toothpaste. A magnet can push or pull another magnet. A magnet can also pull a **magnetic material**.

Repulsion and Attraction

Magnetic **repulsion** happens when a magnet pushes away, or repels, another magnet. Magnetic **attraction** happens when a magnet pulls, or attracts, another magnet or magnetic material. Repulsion and attraction make magnets very useful. Magnets on cupboard doors help them to click shut. Magnets at a junkyard sort magnetic metals from nonmagnetic metals. Magnetic repulsion can lift a maglev train (see page 16) and make it hover above the train tracks.

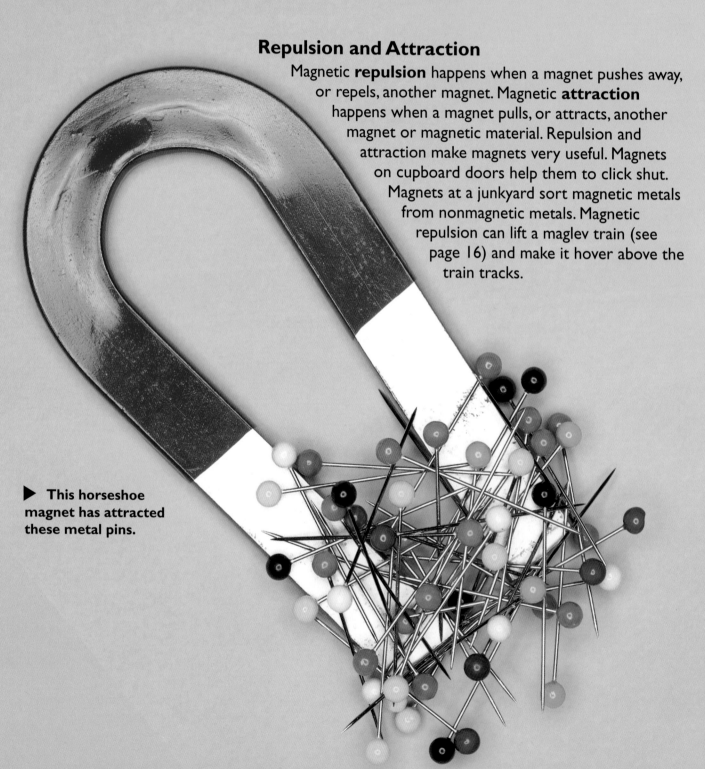

▶ **This horseshoe magnet has attracted these metal pins.**

Magnetic Poles

Every magnet has a north **pole** and a south pole. The magnetism is strongest at the poles. If the north pole of one magnet is held close to the south pole of a second magnet, they will attract each other. If two like poles, such as north and north, are held together, they will repel each other.

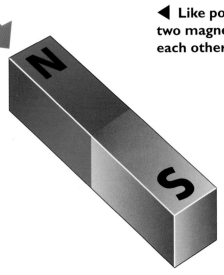

◀ Opposite poles of two magnets attract each other.

Types of Magnet

Magnets come in all shapes, sizes, and strengths. They are often made from iron, nickel, or cobalt metals. Magnetite is a naturally-occurring magnetic rock. Ceramic magnets are powerful and are made of a mixture of chemicals, but they usually contain iron. Magnets can be shaped as bars, horseshoes, rings, and disks. Magnets can even be flexible (bendy).

◀ Like poles of two magnets repel each other.

SCIENCE AT WORK

When a magnet is cut in half, each half has a north and south pole. If the magnet is broken into hundreds of tiny pieces, each piece still has a north and south pole.

Which Materials Are Magnetic?

A magnet will stick to a metal radiator or a refrigerator door, but it will not stick to a wooden table or an aluminum can. Magnets attract magnetic materials. Magnetic materials are always metals. However, not all metals are magnetic.

Magnetic and Nonmagnetic

Iron, nickel, and cobalt are magnetic metals. Any material that contains these metals is also usually magnetic. Steel contains iron, so a magnet will attract a food can made from steel.

Copper, gold, and aluminum are metals, but they are not magnetic. A magnet will not attract a can made from aluminum. Nonmetals, such as paper, wood, plastic, and glass, are also not magnetic.

Magnetic Force

The force of a magnet describes how strongly a magnet can attract a magnetic material. Strong magnets have a greater **magnetic force** than weak magnets. **Electromagnets** are very strong magnets. They have a magnetic force when the electricity passes through them.

❋ **What is the difference between a magnet and a magnetic material?**

◀ **Refrigerator magnets are attracted to the metal in this refrigerator door.**

THE SCIENCE DETECTIVE INVESTIGATES:

Find the Magnetic Materials

You will need:
- 10 small household items
- magnet • notebook
- pen

Collect ten household items. Your collection should include cans, coins, silverware, a selection of different nails, and objects made from glass, rubber, and plastic. Draw a table with two columns "Magnetic" and "Nonmagnetic." Predict which items you think are magnetic and which are nonmagnetic. Write down your predictions. Test your predictions by holding a magnet near each item. Can you feel a magnetic force? Were your predictions correct?

Some of your results may surprise you. Coins that look like they are made from copper may actually be steel disks coated with copper. They will therefore be magnetic. Silverware is often made from steel, but a type of steel called stainless steel is not magnetic. Nails can be made from a variety of metals including iron, aluminum, stainless steel, or brass.

What Is a Magnetic Field?

When you hold two magnets near each other, you can feel the repulsion or attraction. This magnetic force can be felt in an area around the magnet. The area is called the **magnetic field**. If the magnet is weak, the magnetic field is small. If the magnet is strong, the magnetic field is large.

Detecting Magnetic Fields

It is impossible to know where a magnetic field is by looking at a magnet. To discover where the magnetic field is, we need either another magnet or a magnetic material. **Iron filings** are tiny pieces of iron metal. They are magnetic. When iron filings are sprinkled around a bar magnet, they arrange themselves into lines. The lines travel out of the top of the magnet, and loop around to the bottom of the magnet. The lines show the magnetic field.

The magnetic field of a horseshoe magnet looks different. One end of the magnet is the north pole and one is the south pole. Iron filings form lines that connect the two poles.

▼ Lines of magnetic force show the magnetic field. The lines join the two poles.

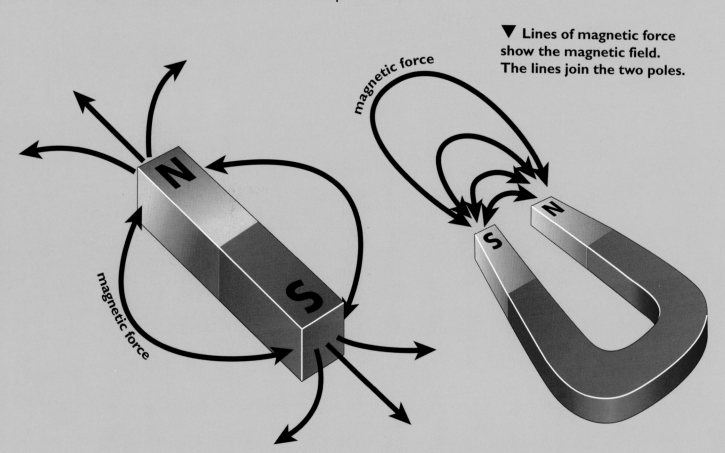

magnetic force

magnetic force

THE SCIENCE DETECTIVE INVESTIGATES:

The Power of Magnetism

You will need:
• bar magnet • iron filings • thin paper • thick card • hardback book

Magnetic fields can pass through air, but can they pass through a solid such as paper? Follow the instructions to investigate magnetic fields.

1 Sprinkle iron filings onto a piece of paper.
2 Carefully lift the paper with one hand.
3 Hold a magnet directly beneath the iron filings, touching the paper, and slowly move the magnet. Do the iron filings move?
4 Repeat the procedure using a piece of card and then a book instead of paper. What happens? What conclusions can you draw?
5 Next, place the bar magnet on a piece of paper.
6 Sprinkle the iron filings around the magnet. What happens? Can you see any lines of the magnetic field?

🐾 **Through which materials can magnetism not pass?**

SCIENCE AT WORK

No one knows for sure when magnetism was first discovered. The most common legend tells of a shepherd named Magnes who lived 4,000 years ago. He lived in a part of Greece called Magnesia. One day, Magnes was herding his sheep when his metal-tipped staff became stuck to a large black rock. The nails in his shoes also became stuck. The magnetic rock was named magnetite after either the area Magnesia, or the shepherd, Magnes.

▶ **This is magnetite, Earth's naturally occurring magnetic rock. It attracts magnetic materials.**

Is the Earth a Magnet?

Our planet has a north and a south pole, just like a magnet. If you could see them, the Earth's magnetic lines of force would loop around from the North Pole to the South Pole. This would look similar to the lines of force created by a bar magnet.

The Earth's Magnetic Field

The outer surface of the Earth is rocky, but at the center of the Earth there is a solid core of iron. As the Earth spins, liquid iron swirls around the core. This creates a magnetic field. The Sun releases dangerous particles into space, which speed toward Earth at 248 miles (400 km) per second. The Earth's magnetic field protects the Earth from these particles by not allowing them to enter the Earth's **atmosphere**.

Compasses

A **compass** needle aligns itself with the Earth's magnetic field. This means that it always points in a north to south direction. By turning a compass until the needle points at the "N" for "north" you know exactly where north, south, east, and west are located.

▼ **Magnetism is created by the spinning of the Earth's core. It forms a magnetic field around the Earth.**

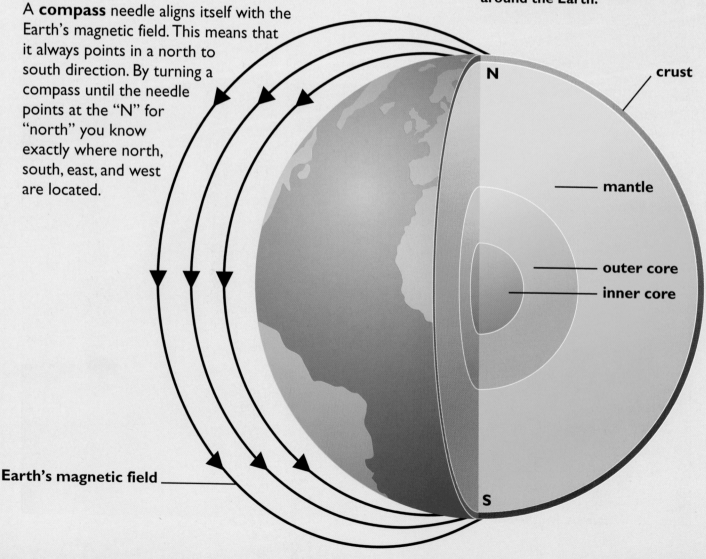

crust

mantle

outer core

inner core

Earth's magnetic field

THE SCIENCE DETECTIVE INVESTIGATES:

Magnets and Compasses

You will need:
• compass • bar magnet • pencil • large sheet of paper

Investigate the effect of a magnet on a compass.

1 Place the magnet on a plain sheet of paper and draw around it.
2 Put the compass at the end of the north pole of the magnet.
3 Draw a cross (x) at the far end of the needle (marked A in the diagram).
4 Move the compass on the paper until the other end of the needle points
   directly to the cross (marked A).
5 Draw another cross at the far end of the needle (marked B in the diagram).
6 Continue this process, marking each time where the far end of the needle is,
   until you reach the south pole of the magnet or you run out of paper.
   Connect the crosses. You have drawn along a line of magnetic force.

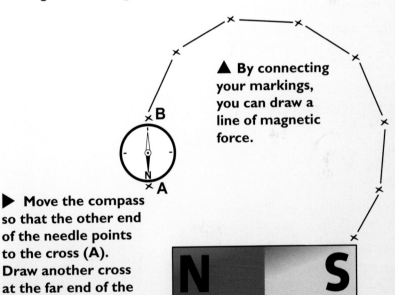

▲ **By connecting your markings, you can draw a line of magnetic force.**

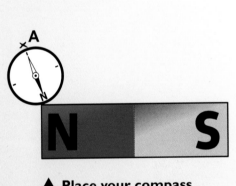

▲ **Place your compass at the north pole of the magnet. Draw a cross at the other end of the needle (A).**

▶ **Move the compass so that the other end of the needle points to the cross (A). Draw another cross at the far end of the needle (B).**

SCIENCE AT WORK

William Gilbert (1544–1603) was a scientist who is described as the founder of the science of magnetism. In one of his experiments, he made a mini Earth out of magnetic rock. He used the mini Earth to show that a compass needle not only points north, but also dips toward north, exactly following the Earth's lines of magnetic force.

Are Magnets All the Same?

Magnets come in different shapes, sizes, and strengths. Long, thin magnets hold cupboard doors shut, flexible magnets are often used for refrigerator magnets and strong electromagnets are found in machines such as **motors**, scanners, and doorbells.

Strength and Size

The size of a magnet does not tell you how strong it is. Tiny magnets can be extremely strong, and large magnets are not always as powerful as you might think. Electromagnets are usually stronger than ordinary magnets.

What Is an Electromagnet?

When electricity travels through a wire, it creates a magnetic field in the wire. If the wire is wrapped around a metal object, such as a nail, the nail becomes an electromagnet. The magnetic field is only present when the electricity is switched on. If it is turned off, the magnetism goes away.

Uses of Electromagnets

Electromagnets are more useful than ordinary magnets because the magnetism can be turned on and off. MRI (magnetic resonance imaging) scanners contain extremely powerful electromagnets. They use magnetism and **radio waves** to look inside the human body. They can detect differences between types of tissue in the body. They can tell the difference between muscle and bone, for example.

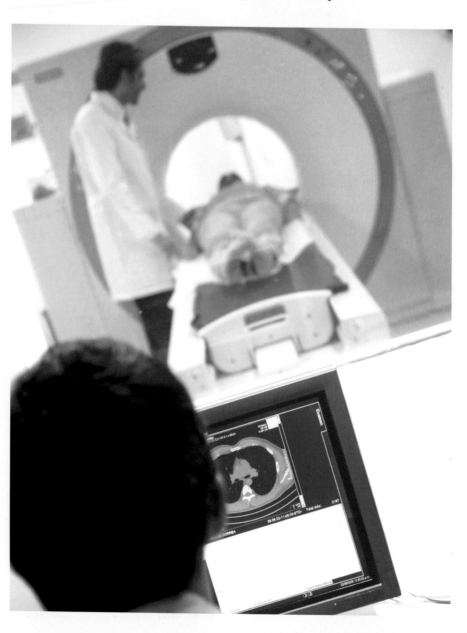

▼ **The patient lies on a table inside the scanner. The scanner creates an image on a screen to show the inside of the patient's body.**

THE SCIENCE DETECTIVE INVESTIGATES:

Which Magnet Is the Strongest?

You will need
• 5 or 6 magnets • 100 metal paper clips of the same size

Use your detective skills and the information here to investigate magnet strength.

1 Number your magnets and draw a table to record your results. The table headings should read "Magnet" and "Number of paper clips."
2 Hold a paper clip so that it just touches the first magnet. Slowly let go. The paper clip should cling to the magnet.
3 Take another paper clip and hold it so that it just touches the first paper clip. Slowly let go.
4 Repeat step 3 until you reach a paper clip that will not cling on.
5 Write down how many paper clips the magnet holds. Note: Only the first paper clip should touch the magnet.
6 Repeat steps 2–5 with each magnet. It is important to use a new set of paper clips with each magnet.

It is likely that each magnet held a different number of paper clips. The magnet that held the most paper clips is the strongest. The magnet that held the fewest paper clips is the weakest. What conclusions can you draw from your experiment? Do you think that size and shape affect magnet strength?

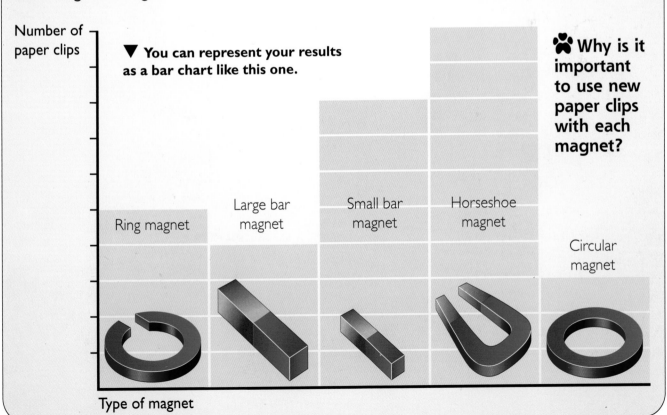

Number of paper clips

▼ You can represent your results as a bar chart like this one.

Ring magnet

Large bar magnet

Small bar magnet

Horseshoe magnet

Circular magnet

🐾 Why is it important to use new paper clips with each magnet?

Type of magnet

How Do We Use Magnets?

Electric motors, speakers, and doorbells are a small selection of the vast number of machines that contain magnets. Without magnets, our homes would be dark because there would be no electricity. Hospitals would find it difficult to diagnose patients because medical scanners would not work, and everyone would have to use cash because credit cards are made with a magnetic strip.

Recycling

Waste steel can be **recycled** into new steel products. A large, powerful electromagnet attracts steel cans, separating them from the rest of the garbage. They are crushed into large cubes and taken to a steel mill. Here they are combined with other steel waste, such as steel from cars and construction. The steel is melted together to make new steel.

▼ **The scrap metal at this recycling center is being lifted by a large magnet.**

Credit Cards

The backs of credit cards, travel tickets, and identification cards contain a strip called a magnetic stripe. The stripe contains lots of tiny magnetic particles, each one too tiny to see. The particles can be made to point in either a north or south pole direction. This forms a code that contains lots of information. When a credit card is swiped, the machine reads information held in the stripe, such as the account number, the name of the card owner, and how much they can spend using the card.

SCIENCE AT WORK

Animals such as turtles, fish, and some bats use the Earth's magnetic field to guide them over long distances. Some fish even have sensors made from magnetic materials in their bodies. Baby loggerhead turtles hatch on sandy beaches. They crawl toward the ocean and swim for more than 9,000 miles (15,000 km) over several years before they return to the coast on which they were born. They do this by following the Earth's magnetic field.

▶ **Newly-hatched loggerhead turtles are only 2 in. (5 cm) long, but they are still able to find their way using the Earth's magnetism.**

How Do Trains Use Magnetism?

Many of us have traveled on ordinary trains. These trains have wheels that run along a track. However, not all trains have wheels. Maglev trains have extremely powerful magnets instead of wheels. They levitate (hover) above a **guideway** as they zoom along.

How Trains Hover

Magnets are attached to the underneath of maglev trains. As the train moves along at high speed, electromagnets in the guideway repel (push) the magnets and lift the train. Many ordinary trains are powered by engines that burn diesel fuel. Maglev trains do not have engines. Instead, the magnetic fields in the guideway not only lift the train, they also pull and push it along.

🐾 **What do you think "maglev" is short for?**

▼ **The Shanghai maglev railroad in China was the first maglev train to take paying customers.**

New Maglev Technology

In Japan, engineers are developing maglev trains that use even more powerful electromagnets. These magnets operate at supercooled (extremely cold) temperatures. They save **energy** and lift the train almost 4 in. (10 cm) above the guideway—higher than older maglev trains. The trains roll on rubber tires until they reach their takeoff speed of 62 miles (100 km) per hour.

SCIENCE AT WORK

- Maglev trains levitate from 0.39–3.93 in. (1–10 cm) above the guideway.
- There is no **friction** between the maglev train and the guideway. As a result, these trains can travel up to 310 miles (500 km) per hour.
- The first maglev passenger train ran in 2003 in Shanghai, China.
- Germany, China, and Japan have the most advanced plans for future high-speed maglev railroads.

THE SCIENCE DETECTIVE INVESTIGATES:

Hovering Magnets

You will need:
• plasticine • pencil • 6 ceramic doughnut magnets (make sure that the pencil just fits into the hole in the magnets)

Investigate the hovering power of magnets.

1 Form a ball of plasticine and press it on a table.
2 Insert a pencil into the plasticine.
3 Drop a doughnut magnet down the pencil so that south is facing up.
4 Take a second magnet and drop it down the pencil so that south is facing down. The top magnet should hover over the bottom magnet. If you do not know which is north and south, you will need to hold the magnets near each other to find out which side repels the first magnet.
5 Take a third magnet and drop it down so that north is facing down.
6 Repeat this process with the remaining magnets, making sure each time that like poles are facing.

Your magnets hover because of the power of magnetic repulsion.

▲ **When like poles are facing, the magnets should hover like this.**

What Is a Spring?

Springs can make our lives more comfortable. They make our mattresses soft and give us a smooth ride in our cars. Springs are useful in other ways, too. They pull doors shut, make some types of clock work, and are found in many toys.

▲ Springs come in all shapes and sizes, depending on the job that they do.

Stretched and Squashed

A spring is a coil of material, usually metal. When the two ends are pushed inward, the coils move closer together. If the spring is suddenly let go, it will ping back to its original shape. When the ends of a spring are pulled apart, the coils move farther apart. If it is let go, it will go back to its original shape.

THE SCIENCE DETECTIVE INVESTIGATES:

Spring Search

You will need:
• notebook • pen

Investigate your home to find as many springs as possible. Draw a table with the following headings: Device, Number of springs, Purpose of the spring(s). Start by looking for springs inside your home. Check doors, chairs, and toys. Check items on your desk and the contents of your pencil case. Next, if you have a yard, go outside. Check gardening tools, bikes, and gates. Write down your findings. In some cases, you will not be able to see the springs, but you may be able to tell that they are there. For example, most mattresses contain springs and we know this because the mattress is bouncy.

Mattress Springs

Many modern mattresses
contain steel springs. These
are called coil springs, or
coils. The thickness of the
metal in the coil affects how
bouncy or firm the mattress
feels. Thick metal coils can
not be easily squashed and
make the mattress very firm.
Thinner ones can be
squashed more easily and
make the mattress softer.

SCIENCE AT WORK

Coiled springs were
first used in door
locks around 500
years ago. A bolt kept
the door shut and was
held in place by a
spring. To open the
door, a key turned and
squashed the spring.
The bolt moves back
and the door opens.

► A trampoline has
an elastic sheet that is
connected to the frame
by springs.

What Happens When You Stretch or Compress a Spring?

Pogo sticks are toys that contain a spring. When you bounce up and down on a pogo stick, the two ends of the spring are pushed together and then move apart. We say that the spring **compresses** and **stretches**. As it does so, it creates a force that bounces you into the air.

THE SCIENCE DETECTIVE INVESTIGATES:

Changing Bands

You will need:
• small and large rubber band of the same thickness • 2 rubber bands of the same size but different thickness

Rubber bands can be stretched in the same way as a spring. Gently stretch the first small rubber band. Be aware that it may snap back painfully, so keep it well away from your face. Can you feel the forces on your fingers? Now stretch the large rubber band. Does the force feel the same for the two rubber bands? Next, compare the second two rubber bands in the same way. How does the force vary between the rubber bands? Do size and thickness affect the force that a rubber band exerts?

◀ The harder you bounce on a pogo stick, the higher it will throw you up into the air.

Spring Forces

Imagine a spring placed on a hard surface. When you push down on the spring and compress it, you feel the spring push into your hand. The spring exerts an upward force on your hand. The same thing happens with a pogo stick. When the person jumps, the spring compresses and then pushes up. The spring always wants to return to its original shape. A spring stuck to the underside of a table will also exert forces. If you push up on the spring and compress it, the spring's force pushes downward.

Spring Energy

A compressed spring or a stretched spring has stored energy. When it is released, it uses this energy to change back into its original shape. The stored energy can also move an object such as a gate. When the gate is opened, the spring stretches and stores energy. When the gate is let go, the spring returns to its original shape and pulls the gate shut.

🐾 **When a rubber band is stretched downward, in which direction does it exert a force?**

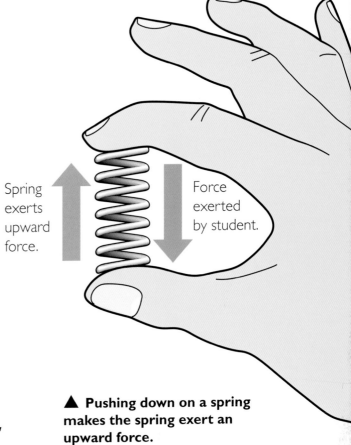

Spring exerts upward force.

Force exerted by student.

▲ **Pushing down on a spring makes the spring exert an upward force.**

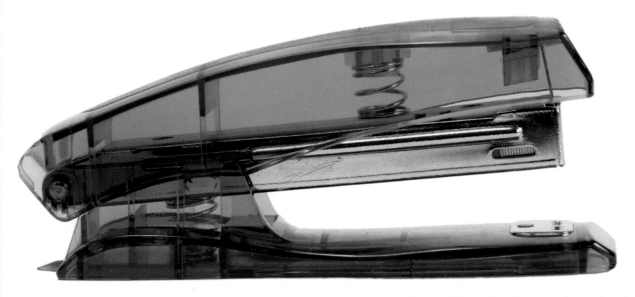

▲ **A stretched spring in a stapler holds the staples in position. Another spring is compressed when you squeeze the stapler together.**

Why Are Spring-Loaded Objects Useful?

If you have ever clicked the end of a pen to make the tip come out, then you have used a **spring-loaded** object. In spring-loaded objects, the spring moves part of the object or holds part of it in position. In the pen, a spring tries to push the tip back in, but a catch holds it in place. You press a button on the pen to release the spring and the tip moves back in.

Toasters

In a toaster, a spring-loaded tray pops the toast out. By pushing the handle, a spring is stretched and the bread moves down into the toaster. The heater cooks the toast and when it is ready, the heater switches off. The spring is released and out pops the toast.

SCIENCE AT WORK

In the early nineteenth century, a Frenchman named Antoine Gibus invented a spring-loaded top hat. Top hats were very tall. People sitting behind someone wearing a top hat at the theater could not see the stage. Gibus' hat contained thin metal springs. It could be squashed flat and stored under the theater seat. A quick shake and the hat would spring open again.

▶ The springs in a toaster exert an upward force to pop up the toast.

Umbrellas

Umbrellas can be spring loaded. When the umbrella is closed, the spring inside the handle is compressed. To open the umbrella, you press a button, the spring extends, and the umbrella opens.

◀ **To close a spring-loaded umbrella, push the two ends of the umbrella together to compress the spring. When it clicks, a catch has moved to hold the spring in place and keep the umbrella closed.**

Nail Guns

A nail gun is a tool used to fire a nail into a piece of wood. This makes jobs such as nailing down floorboards much quicker and easier. In a spring-loaded nail gun, pulling the trigger compresses a spring and pulls back a nail. When the spring suddenly stretches again, it fires out the nail at high speed. It is important never to touch a nail gun because they can be very dangerous.

▲ **This spring-loaded nail gun is being used to secure wood to the outside of a house.**

How Are Springs Used in Measuring?

You may have a **spring scale** in your bathroom or own a watch that is wound by hand. Spring scales and **spring balances** measure **mass**. Clocks and watches measure time. Springs are an essential part of these measuring devices.

▲ **Bathroom scales**

Heavy or Light

Some bathroom scales have a large dial around which a marker moves. When you stand on the scale, a lever inside the scale pulls downward on the stiff spring. This movement turns a marker that points to your mass. Mass is usually measured in pounds or kilograms.

Weighing Fish

Anglers use spring balances to weigh their catch. The harder a spring is pulled, the more it will stretch. In a spring balance fish scale, a hook hangs down from a dial. The dial looks like the one on the bathroom scale. An angler hangs the fish from the hook. The heavier the fish, the more a spring stretches inside the dial, and the farther it moves the marker around the dial. The mass can be read from the dial.

▲ **An angler weighs his catch on a spring balance.**

Clockwork

Springs are not always shaped like long **cylinders**. Flat springs spiral out from the center instead of spiraling downward. These springs are found in some watches and **clockwork** toys. The springs can be tightly wound and as they gradually unwind, they make the clock's hands move, or make the toy work.

▶ **The springs in clockwork devices are flat. When they are wound tightly, the coils are pressed together. As they unwind, the coils move apart.**

SCIENCE AT WORK

Some radios do not need **batteries** or **household electricity** to work. Instead, they can be powered by human muscle. Clockwork radios are wound up by hand. As they are wound, a spring is coiled tightly. The spring slowly unwinds and turns a **generator** that powers the radio. These radios are useful in remote places where there is little access to other sources of electricity.

◀ **This San Bushman (tribesman) is listening to his clockwork windup radio in the Kalahari Desert, Africa.**

How Are Springs Used in Suspension?

Look at the road outside your house. It probably looks smooth but most roads are actually covered with small bumps, ridges, and stones. So why does the road feel smooth when you ride in a moving car? Cars have **suspension** systems that connect the wheels to the body of the car. The suspension cushions you from the bumps in the road.

How Car Suspension Works

Suspension systems contain springs. When a car tire travels over a bump in the road, the wheel moves up. When it travels over a hole in the road, the wheel moves down. Without a suspension system, the whole car would move up and down, you would feel every bump, and the trip would be uncomfortable. Springs in the suspension allow the wheels to move up and down but they stop the whole car from moving up and down. The springs cushion the bumps in the road.

▼ Racing cars need good suspension to help them stick to the road as they travel around bends at high speed.

SCIENCE AT WORK

A car's handling describes how well it responds to the driver's control. When a car quickly travels around a corner, you have probably felt yourself being pulled toward the outside of the bend. The car's suspension helps it to "stick" to the road and handle the bends better. The stiffer the suspension springs, the better the handling of the car.

Bike Suspension

Bike suspension systems connect the wheels to the frame. Off-road riding is very bumpy but suspension makes it easier. The springs in the suspension work in a similar way to car suspension. They allow the wheels to move up and down but keep the frame and the rider much more stationary.

▼ **This mountain bike has spring suspension attached to the front wheel.**

▲ **The springs on this quad bike's suspension cushion the rider from the uneven ground.**

Your Project:
Make a Compass

Compass needles are magnets. They point in a north to south direction and help people find their way from place to place. Use this information and your detective skills to make your own magnet and compass.

You will need:
- pin or needle
- bar magnet
- bowl—do not use a metal bowl
- water
- cork
- real compass

Method
1 With one hand, hold the needle by one end. With your other hand, wipe one end of the magnet along the length of the needle in a single movement. Lift up the magnet and wipe it along the needle again in exactly the same way.
2 Continue to wipe the magnet along the needle until you have done so 30 times. It is very important to only wipe the magnet in one direction.
3 Carefully push the needle through the cork. Keep your fingers away from the sharp end of the needle.
4 Fill the bowl with water.
5 Gently place the needle and cork on the water. It should float. After a few minutes, the needle will rotate so that it points in a north to south direction. Keep your equipment well away from metal, electrical, and magnetic devices.

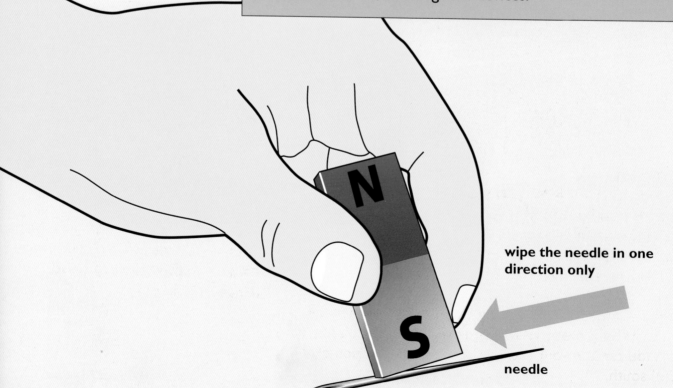

wipe the needle in one direction only

needle

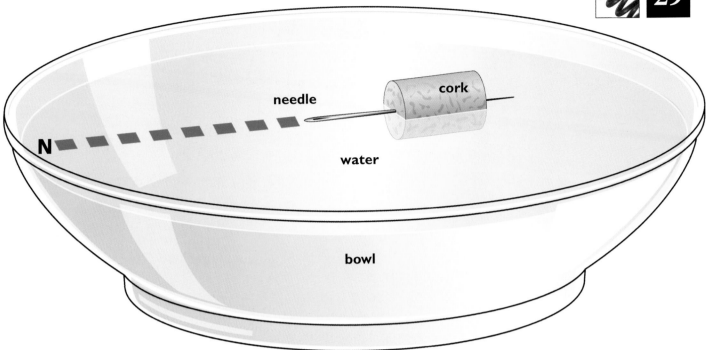

▲ Closely watch the floating needle to see how it turns.

◀ Check to see if your water compass points in the same direction as a real compass.

What Happened and Why?

Everything is made up of tiny particles that are too small to see. These particles are called atoms. When the magnet is wiped along the needle, it causes all of the needle's atoms to line up and point in the same direction. This makes the needle magnetic.

When the needle floats in water, it can turn freely. It aligns itself with the Earth's magnetic field and points in a north to south direction. You can use your compass to find the direction of north and south.

🐾 Why is it important to keep your compass away from metal, electrical, and magnetic devices?

Glossary

angler A fisherman.

atmosphere The layer of gases that surround planet Earth.

attraction The force that pulls two objects together.

battery A portable device that contains chemicals and produces electricity.

clockwork A device that is driven by a spring. When a clockwork device is wound, a spring becomes tightly coiled. As the spring unwinds, it powers the device.

compass A device that uses magnetism to locate north, south, east, and west

compress To squash.

cylinder A tube-shaped object. Cylinders have circular ends and straight parallel sides. They can be hollow or solid.

electromagnet A very powerful magnet that only works when the electricity is switched on.

energy The ability to do work.

force A push or a pull.

friction A type of force that tries to stop an object from moving. There is friction between a car's wheels and the road.

generator A machine that creates electricity.

guideway A path along which maglev trains travel.

household electricity Electricity that is supplied to homes, offices, and schools through a grid system. A grid system consists of cables connected in a large network that spreads out across a large area.

iron filings Tiny pieces of iron metal that look like a dark powder.

magnetic field The area around a magnet in which its force can be detected.

magnetic force The strength with which a magnet can attract another magnet or magnetic material.

magnetic material A substance that can be attracted by a magnet.

mass The amount of matter in an object.

motor A type of machine or engine that creates movement.

pole The ends of a magnet are its poles.

radio wave A wave of energy. Radio waves carry radio and television signals, and are used in MRI scanners.

recycle To reuse something again.

repulsion The force that pushes two objects apart.

spring A coil of material, usually metal.

spring balance A device that contains a spring that measures mass. When an object is weighed, the spring is stretched downward.

spring loaded A spring-loaded object contains a spring that presses one part against another and holds the parts in position.

spring scale A device that contains a spring that measures mass. An object is weighed by placing it on the scale.

stretch To grow longer. When springs are stretched, their coils move apart from each other.

suspension A system in a vehicle that cushions the passenger from bumps in the road.

Answers

Page 6: A magnet attracts magnetic materials. A magnetic material is attracted to a magnet but doesn't attract other magnetic materials.

Page 7: Some items—such as glasses, wooden spoons, rubber bands, pencils, and mugs—will be nonmagnetic. Other items—such as steel cans, paper clips, thumbtacks, and some keys—will be magnetic.

Page 9: The iron filings should move and follow the magnet. The magnetism is able to pass through the sheet of paper. Depending on the strength of the magnet, the magnetism might pass through the card. Most household magnets are not strong enough for the magnetism to pass through a hardback book. When iron filings are sprinkled around a magnet, they should collect on the lines of the magnetic field.

Page 9: It is possible for magnetism to pass through any substance that is not magnetic. For example, magnetism can pass through air, water, paper, wood, aluminum, copper, glass, and brass.

Page 11: When a magnet is held next to a compass, the compass needle swings and aligns itself with the lines of magnetic force.

Page 13: Example answer: The horseshoe magnet held the most paper clips. The circular magnet held the fewest paper clips. We can conclude that size does not affect the strength of a magnet in this investigation, but shape does affect the strength of a magnet.

Page 13: It is important to use new paper clips every time because the paper clips may become magnetised when used. By using new paper clips, we make sure that we conduct a fair test.

Page 16: Maglev is short for "magnetic levitation."

Page 18: Example answer: In your home, you may find springs in the base of a chair, a mattress, and a stapler. In your yard, you may find springs in a gate, a patio chair, and a hand pruner (a type of garden scissors).

Page 20: When you stretch a rubber band, it exerts forces on your fingers in the opposite direction. Smaller, thicker rubber bands usually exert greater forces than larger, thinner rubber bands.

Page 21: When a rubber band is stretched downward, it exerts an upward force.

Page 29: Magnetic, electrical, and some metal devices distort a compass reading. They create their own magnetic fields. The compass will detect this magnetic field, react to it, and no longer point in a true north to south direction.

Further Reading and Web Sites

Books

Junior Scientists: Experiment With Magnets
by Christine Taylor-Butler
(Cherry Lake Publishing, 2010)

Magnetism: An Investigation
by John Stringer
(PowerKids Press, 2008)

Science Alive: Magnet
by Terry J. Jennings
(Smart Apple Media, 2008)

Web Sites

For Web resources related to the subject of this book, go to: http://www.windmillbooks.com/weblinks and select this book's title.

Index

The numbers in **bold** refer to pictures